"With startling ease and quiet artistry, these poems hone in on the heat signatures of cruelty and belonging, memory and creation, belief and unknowing. Rose experiences God's voice as 'singing bruises' and identifies feelings that 'bypass the brain.' About a third of the way in, she confides: 'I don't know how to write; I only know how to strip back bark to see if I'm still green on the inside.' Oh, how she does, and is!"—Ellen Doré Watson, author of *pray me stay eager*

ONCE, THIS FOREST BELONGED TO A STORM

ONCE, THIS FOREST BELONGED TO A STORM

AUSTEN LEAH ROSE

University of Massachusetts Press
Amherst and Boston

Copyright © 2023 by University of Massachusetts Press

Printed in the United States of America

ISBN 978-1-62534-727-5 (paper)

Designed by Deste Roosa
Set in Freight Text Pro and Neue Haas Grotesk
Printed and bound by Books International, Inc.

Cover design by adam b. bohannon
Cover photo by Michael Schweppes, *Redwood National Forest*, 2005. CCBY-SA 2.0;
https://creativecommons.org/licenses/by-sa/2.0/.

Library of Congress Cataloging-in-Publication Data
Names: Rose, Austen Leah, 1987– author.
Title: Once, this forest belonged to a storm / Austen Leah Rose.
Description: Amherst : University of Massachusetts Press, [2023] | Series:
    Juniper Prize for Poetry
Identifiers: LCCN 2022045025 (print) | LCCN 2022045026 (ebook) | ISBN
    9781625347275 (paperback) | ISBN 9781685750206 (ebook)
Subjects: LCGFT: Poetry.
Classification: LCC PS3618.O782827 O53 2023 (print) | LCC PS3618.O782827
    (ebook) | DDC 811/.6--dc23/eng/20220926
LC record available at https://lccn.loc.gov/2022045025
LC ebook record available at https://lccn.loc.gov/2022045026

British Library Cataloguing-in-Publication Data
A catalog record for this book is available from the British Library.

CONTENTS

ONCE, THIS FOREST BELONGED TO A STORM

Nocturne

At night, the windows in our house
become mirrors, as if to say

what happens here will keep on happening.

I press my face to the glass
and see
black trees, black sky, the moon like a pocket

turned inside out.

Below, I hear
a howl, which means our mother is dreaming
with her eyes open

again. I don't go downstairs after dark

but sometimes
I talk to God from my bedroom.

His voice sounds
like pink and blue buds opening inside of me,
like singing bruises.

Theory of Nature

I

I spent most of my days alone

peeling apart the fibrous stems of meadowfoam, chewing wild mint, applying
aloe to my cuts and scrapes.

In the afternoon, the sunlight split like an overripe lemon. The olive tree
dropped its fruit along the driveway. Acrid, inedible.

Sometimes, my sister and I went on walks, collecting carob pods
in our back pockets, stumbling over the bumps in the asphalt
raised by thirsty root systems of pine and eucalyptus.

If your second toe is bigger than your first toe, my sister said, it means
you're a lesbian. We would say anything before admitting

what we didn't know. The only naked bodies we'd ever seen
were at Hebrew school: images from the Holocaust projected at midday

on a white screen. In the evening, wind. Palm fronds
brushed the side of the house like an instrument. Fan-shaped, frost-tender.
Downstairs, my mother poured herself a drink.

I was developing my own theory of nature:

my body, I believed, was a greenhouse and, sometimes, rare orchids pressed
their two-toned tendrils against the glass.

I spoke the language of minuscule increments: a drop of dew absorbed
by the span of a single green leaf. An alteration to the oxygen level,
imperceptible to any human or insect.

II

In moonlight, caterpillars hang upside down from the leaves
of the lemon tree; the bougainvillea turns vermilion. You drift
into a milky weather made of murmuring,

which is the voice of grownups, somewhere far away and full of plans.

Across the hall, your sister sleeps like a dove egg, complete in her loneliness;
a pair of yellow owl eyes clicks open in the thinning pine.

Soon you will be thirteen. You will walk down the aisles of your synagogue,
carry four thousand years of history wrapped in white silk
with blue embroidery,

watch your mother vomit on her silver sequined dress.

Forget the diamond-backed design of the rattlesnake.
Forget the gold shrub with its shiny red berries. Forget the decadent heat
of July.

In summer, the clover halts its growing, then goes dormant, then dead.

It's like, one day you're opening a bedroom window to let in the breeze
and the next day you don't know where the window is, how to open it, why
you would even want to.

Threat from Above

First, we saw smoke, then the whole thing
tipped, like a glass of milk,

       and met the hillside. How unlikely;
       as if the sky had made a promise

it couldn't keep. That day
the brush was so dry it creaked;

       I pressed my ear to the ground
       and heard the muffled shouts

of a man and woman arguing
like an ocean in a conch shell.

       At once, everything
       I touched turned slippery.

Rarely do we know the names
for things that happen to us.

       That night, we collected bits of the wreckage
       caught in the moonlight like silver minnows.

Morbid, our parents said when
we made them into jewelry.

The Cruelty of Language

Last week, when you were in the hospital, I had to repeat to myself in the parking lot that *I* was not *you*, had to let language pry us apart, like a knife, cruel but necessary.

The Visit

The assignment was to be brave.
The instructions were to enter through the front door.
               Here, sunlight
shows up unannounced on the side of a grieving woman's
face. There is a glass of water on a metal tray
and a number on a machine
measuring how the heart will beat despite its suffering.
Don't speak; the body has its own language.
Your throat is a pond frozen overnight.
Your knees are two sparrows trembling on an icy branch.
Through the square window you see a parking lot framed by
melting snow, pine, dried bramble the color
of baked bread, which you take to mean winter, daytime, north,
evidence that even this moment is a point on a line
stretching far in opposite directions.
You see your sister propped on a pillow in a narrow cot
and you know wherever it is a poem comes from,
it's the same place you feel pierced now,
in the middle of your spine, her pain talking to your pain,
the way you each used to knock on a shared bedroom wall
to signal that all was not all right.

The Outlaw

I don't go into town anymore.

I bring out the emergency in people and I don't know why.

When I speak women fall sick and stars drop like dead birds from the night.

My home, instead, is on a ridge where horses bow their heads
and bear the elements.

Alone, I conduct experiments. I communicate with storms. I stack stones
and make signs that only I can understand.

Is it possible to love the world so much it pushes you away?

My silence has a shape; a mirage in the desert.

I have learned to sit so still I can make my heart stop.

Notes on Flying

Birds fly, airplanes fly, superheroes fly, it's common
for children to dream about flying, they say fear
of flying is Fear of the Unknown, but I think
it's Fear of What I Know But Wish I Didn't. Flying
is the farthest you will ever be from home. In ancient times
flying meant you had entered the realm of the gods.
Angels fly. Time flies. Some people say making love feels like
flying, a losing track of your limbs. Millions of years ago
penguins flew. In my dreams I stand on a balcony
in a white nightgown, the wind is rifling through the tops
of palm trees and I fly over a city; the city is mine, it belongs to me
with its tiny pink lights flickering on off all night,
the silent score of human life. It feels like my father
carrying me upstairs into bed, a time when closeness
was permissible, his scratchy face on my face, his rough, red hands.
At the beach, people bury the ones they love so they won't
fly away. Flying is the opposite of dying—or maybe it's the same.
Flying cars, flying saucers, flying country songs that tell you
to drive and keep on driving, there are no bounds
in flying, no tops or bottoms to it, no men with perfectly reasonable
explanations. Let me tell you: there is nothing sadder
than watching someone try to fly who can't. Flapping
their arms helplessly like a fool, jumping off chairs,
hopping around the apartment. It's a very private matter,
flying, done only at night, in disguise, or by formal invitation.
The bird that forgets it's a bird. Somewhere between earth
and the sky, the beginning and end of an era.

Memory #1

She'd been drinking again. She fumbled with her phone, turned down a dead end, drove uneasily through a dark alley.

Outside, a white fence, useless against the hill's erosion. I rolled down the car window.

Always this divide, this sheet of glass convincing me that what is is only in my mind.

San Fernando Valley, 1999

I see you down there, under a cellophane of stars,

pink sting of sunset,
plate of grilled corn, city lights blinking like the eyes of cattle
in the distance,

mother shouting, sister running

away, the faces of your family growing dim in the approaching dark,
less human, more mask-like.

You look down at your hands, which appear to belong to you
but are useless, clumsy.

What do you call a secret you keep mostly from yourself?

Even at that time, you possessed
a knowledge
that the moment was moving, a feeling

that your chest was a train station which the night ran through.

Then it's daylight
and the world is a wound—rivers, trees, people with literal hearts,
unhidden.

The clouds pass in a series of unexplained silences.

Getting Ready

There was a time when memory was theory,
        before we knew the shapes of constellations,
or fifteen tips for maintaining a relationship, before
        weather patterns, before meaning, when my sister
used to call me to her room while she got dressed.
        Sometimes the world feels like a flash
from an old-fashioned camera. I would sit down on her bed,
        next to her latest boyfriend, with hands
tucked under my legs, and eyes like two dark holes
        widening inside my head. Sometimes I find myself
in places and I don't know how I got there.
        Together we would watch as she took off her shirt,
her naked body bright and buzzing. Like something
        that would shock you if you touched it. Sometimes
I don't know where to look when I'm at a crowded party.
        I remember I could feel his gaze, I could see it
tossed across the room, like a ream of paper.
        Sometimes dreaming is a lot like watching television.
On which side of that secret did I stand.
        Was I my sister. Was I *him*. Who did my eyes belong to.
Sometimes I can convince myself of anything.

Dinner Party in Outer Space

How did you arrive here
with your own fork
and white plate, placed
on a white tablecloth in front of you.

Across is a woman,
tall with a wide face.
She looks like somebody's mother.

Others are lifting up and down
their wine glasses,
discussing ordinary topics
like current seasonal vegetables.

No one seems to notice you are in outer space,
and that alone is something worth talking about.

You concentrate on the dishes passed around,
the momentary gleam of knives
like knowing smiles.
Only eye contact like thin, withering rope
keeps you from falling out of orbit.

Some of the other members of the table
are getting along quite well.
Two are even considering marriage.

Another man and woman are enjoying each other
without romantic undertones.

You seal yourself
airtight. Your heart grows louder,
beating in blue-black space.

The Undrowned World

For fourteen years, my sister and I sailed down a river.
She was starboard; I was port. Together, a complete cosmology.

We sailed through meadows of buckwheat and yarrow.
We sailed through valleys of fog.
Sometimes, I went mad and my sister transcribed my gibberish with both hands
on a piece of willow bark
before sending it away in an osprey's beak.
Sometimes, I braided fish bones into her dark hair.

We were trying to establish a point of view, the way water establishes itself
at the base of a waterfall.

At night, I slept and she watched the stars, or I watched the stars
and she slept, or we both watched the stars and neither of us slept,
or the night was cloudy and there were no stars.

I said, moonlight is a form of radical empathy, and she said, distance
is the color blue, and I said, watching an airplane take off is the best cure
for depression. God is a mountain in translation, she said,
and I thought about this for a few days, ultimately nodding in agreement.
At one point, she had a son,
and, like a butterfly, he was born with the memories of our forgotten childhood.

When she said *sister*, I said, *my body like a boulder against your bright pain.*
When she said *love*, I said, *a type of photograph.*
It went on like this for hours. *I know that I know nothing*, the river said.

Every morning, we watched the sunrise over the undrowned world.
Every morning, we reinvented the river.

Unio Mystica

The original Kabbalists believed that our bodies are made of knots which cut us off from parts of ourselves, and we must untie these knots through the practice of meditation which involves reciting unlikely combinations of letters in order to release words from their meanings.

Maybe that's what Paul Celan meant by *Purpurwort,* or purpleword.

But I don't want to write about the Kabbalists, for whom creation was abstract: lines and colors coming into focus in a cosmic void. I want to write about sitting in the hospital parking lot that night, waiting for you.

Helium-fear, even the mountain stripped of earth's citizenship.

Ein Sof

Behind our synagogue there is a room where people gather after services
to eat and talk, but sometimes
I go in there alone while everyone is still in their seats, praying.
The room is large and dark with a wood floor and stacked chairs and an opening
in the middle of the ceiling that lets in light
like the back of an eye, a place of prayer behind a place of prayer.
I am trying to teach myself forgiveness.
I am trying to remember that God is cruel because God is lonely, and aren't we all?
Outside, the day is a confusion of clouds
and people are saying things they don't really mean.
I did not know there was another sky
behind this sky, bigger than I could ever have imagined, and full of stars.

A Difficult Situation

I was walking down the street when my father called.
It was almost completely dark;

the snow was lit as if plugged in.
I told him that my hypothalamus was overactive,

but some days carry their own weight.
My voice rubbed off on the phone like ink.

When I got home, I wanted my stomach to harden to crystal.
I wanted to feel the raw pit of it,

so I invited this boy over. He sat on my couch;
I took off my skin, and put it next to his.

Kafka says it's easier to see yourself from outside your burrow.
I put on a Bessie Smith album.

The boy looked at me, and I looked at the record player
and my body grew in two directions

like a tree. I am often shocked to look in the mirror
and see a beautiful woman.

I am frightened by enlightenment.
I don't want to forget what unknowing is like.

Interrogation

You never talk about your dreams anymore.
You used to talk about your dreams.

      Even the postal service can't hear you.
      All your letters get returned to sender.

You're like the character in that book
who's always calling to check the train schedule.

      Have you ever thrown dirt on a grave,
      the way they do at Jewish funerals?

That will teach you something about participating.
All this talk about the moon, how it's moving

      away from the earth at the same rate our hair grows.
      You're not the witness I thought you were.

Against Daytime

I went down to the river to spend the day with my friends.
I sat on a rock. I opened my book.
My eyes kept moving between the pages of the book and my friends
who were swimming in the river.
Nearby, a family shared a basket of fruit.
The sun was hot. Soon, my legs burned.
Of course the day would hurt me, I thought.
The day doesn't care about me.
The day just takes and takes and offers nothing in return.
As you can see, I felt sorry for myself.
I squinted into the sun.
There was something unsettled about the day.
It was like flecks of gold floating in the river.
It refused to amount to anything.
Imagine a photograph where everyone is looking in a different direction.
That's what the day was like.
This isn't to say the day wasn't beautiful. The water was clear and green
like the eyes of a fortuneteller.
But I had imagined I might speak to the day directly.
That I could have been alone inside the day.
I thought the sky might have selected me to wrap in its blue blanket
and carry away. But the day was indifferent.
It could not send or receive any secret messages.
Its light fell on everyone equally.
I went back to my book. The book was about an unhappy man.
I had not yet gotten to the part
where I learn why he is unhappy. We know so little about each other,
I said to my friends. On this, we all agreed.

Different Kinds of Feelings

There are many different kinds of feelings: joy, sorrow, etc., but there are some feelings which bypass the brain; for instance, when I fell in love with a tree, I simply started standing up straighter, holding my palms skyward to receive sunlight, storing centuries inside my trunk.

In Defense of Daytime

I told my husband I was going out.
I didn't say where. The car was parked under a tree in a halo
    of dust and leaves. Above, birds.

I put the key in the ignition. I liked the car.
I liked how contained it was. I liked that it had its own temperature.
    Its own code of conduct.

Buckle your seatbelt. Adjust the mirrors. The car makes the world
look like lava. Slow-moving. Rising up to meet you
    and then falling back into the earth.

I was out in the afternoon but I had the feeling
of being behind the afternoon. Like an underground aquifer.
    Something I'd tapped into

which represented the flip side of things.
Like when light comes into the room at a slant
    and you realize the person you're talking to is lying.

Like that. Everything released from the prison of its preconception.
I drove to a shop that sold soaps.
    I walked down the street.

The day had stilled, the way tears gather in a person's eyes
but do not fall. I got to thinking about water.
    I have a friend who laughs whenever she's in water.

There's something you should know about me, she said.
I always laugh when I'm in water.
    I got to thinking about unconditional love.

Unconditional is another way of saying no questions
asked, and when I can't ask questions
    I get angry. Last week, I slammed a door in my husband's face.

You're just like your father, my husband said.
There were people drinking wine on the street.
     There was a breeze coming in from the west.

Maybe I was in a foreign country.
Maybe I was in Greece. Maybe I'd been traveling for months
     on a journey to find myself.

Maybe I had my own apartment with a window
that opens onto the ocean where the light
     pours onto my face each morning like in a Renaissance painting

in which a woman is silently reading a letter. It was still afternoon.
I wasn't in a hurry. The other night I dreamt
     I was in an airplane and the engine stopped

but the airplane floated safely down to earth and landed on an island.
It was a dream that could have been bad but ended up good.
     That was the point.

I drove to the lake. The lake was surrounded by a chain-link fence.
Through the fence I could see mountains. I had recently read
     about a composer

who could only write one minute of music
or an opera. Nothing in between.
     The sky was pink and blue and the palm trees were black

and the lights coming on in the houses
were like the sound of broken glass. In the park someone had planted
     native California plants, which calmed my anxiety.

It was the feeling of everything being in its proper place.
On the drive home, a full moon rose in the sky's throat
     like an unholy thought, preventing the earth from speaking.

Dedication

What child doesn't love to learn that you can strip back the bark on a seemingly dead plant to find it still green on the inside, still living? I don't know how to write; I only know how to strip back bark to see if I'm still green on the inside.

The people in my group therapy say I should try referring to myself by nicer nicknames. Little morning glory. Little sleepy eyes. Little turnip. Little potato pancake. I am doing this one day when suddenly here comes William, most literal adversary of my aloneness.

After we fought, I drove east and hiked five miles into a forest.

I love the forest because I could never write a book about it. *Once upon a time there was a forest*, then nothing happens until a breeze blows through Chapter Two. A few hundred pages of roots absorbing nutrients from dense soil.

In the forest, I play a game with myself. It's called Direct Communication with My Heart. No stethoscope required.

Did you know certain insects can see infrared light? Worms may have a truer understanding of the universe because their brains are less complex and therefore engage in less editing and projection than ours do. Most arachnids have six or eight eyes. Six is a good number of times to read a poem. It is the number of sides a snowflake has and the number of points on a Jewish star.

The Hasidim say that you should treat every object you encounter with holiness. I wish I'd known this earlier. O holy toothbrush. O holy glass of water which William placed on the bedside table while I was reading Dostoevsky. O William's index finger which he uses to hold a pencil when he draws a portrait of me, galaxies where my eyes should be.

William, when you married me, you discovered my collection of broken electronics: a broken record player, a carton of scratched CDs. A dowry of brokenness! You're welcome! My greatest fear was, and still is, that you'll think my poems are too sincere, that you'll leave me for someone who doesn't think about the Holocaust after having sex like I do, but does know the meanings of all your favorite Yiddishisms.

You can't empty the ocean with a spoon
If you don't open your mouth a fly won't get in
When a thief kisses you count your teeth

Being with you is like listening to birdsong is a proverb I just made up, which means *your presence is the articulation of varying degrees of distance,* and also, *this poem is dedicated to you*

Dear Husband

Yesterday

I swam into the center of a dark star, the farthest point
from every other point,

the place

where people become shapes along the shore, where a mother
becomes the idea

of a mother, and a sister becomes the idea of a sister.

Here, everything is its opposite: trees, buildings, snow, Thursday, music,
boredom, regret.

Dear husband, I have been writing you letters, then erasing them,
then sending blank pages in the mail
as if to prove you really are
married

to a ghost. I swear

yesterday I dipped my hand in a pool of emptiness
and dragged up a dead dove. Do you realize what cruelty I'm capable of

when you leave me alone like this? Dear husband

I am thinking of a house with yellow curtains in a town that no one visits,
and where it always rains, a child

tying his shoelaces at the bottom
of a staircase.

Not this wind that knocks the power lines down.

Dear husband

yesterday, I unzipped the translucent skin of my tent to watch the mountains
glow pink somewhere
in Arizona. I swear

I saw a spark
ignite between two mirrors that faced each other in a field.

Love Poem

In the dream, I joined a band of hedonists who feasted on coq au vin
and double chocolate cake and romped around the countryside,
breaking things.

Exhausted, I lay down in the dirt, shoulder blades separated by a slab of granite,
the razor's edge of desire and repulsion,

when suddenly
a mathematician started explaining imaginary numbers as *an invisible bridge
required to get from one rational concept to another,*

adding that *love requires absurd faith bordering on delusion,*

then wanted to show me the results of a science experiment proving
willful ignorance was contagious
by isolating the brain chemical that women produce after giving birth.

We were standing on an ocean cliff, the tide pulled back by the moon's
magnetism to reveal a row of crustaceans like teeth,

when I realized, this whole time, you had been living a secret life
as a rhododendron in a lush garden, and I received a letter from you saying
you'd gotten terribly tangled up with the radishes and onions,

blossoming in places you didn't know you could blossom,

but not to worry, you still loved me,
and when I looked at the sky, my Cassiopeia was the mirror image

of your Cassiopeia,
by which I mean, in the dream, I could see two versions of the same story
at once, which made me cry,

and you said, this is why we have to read books,
because of the natural absorbency of paper,
and I said, this is why music is so dangerous.

Dear Husband

Ever since you told me how you wanted to be touched, three nights ago,

we have not touched. We float in and out of rooms.
We each find our own patch of polished sunlight and sit in it while we listen
to the first eight chords

of Beethoven's Symphony No. 5 in C Minor, which is the sound
of not knowing

what comes next. I have been dreaming of a world in which dreams
are forbidden. I have been dreaming in black and white, like in a war,
when there is only sorrow

or joy, and the world lacks gradient. I have learned two facts about the moon
which contradict each other, then opened our bedroom window

to stare into its blank face. Yesterday, I saw wisteria
blooming by a concrete bridge, its purple petals clanging in the dry air,
and I thought about a portrait

of a sleeping woman we once saw minutes before the museum closed.

I remember when we first met; I told you time had broken into a series
of still photographs. What is it about love that makes it feel impossible to feel
continuously?

Dear husband, sometimes I see eternity in the blind drone of noon.

Today I stepped out of the shower, wrapped myself in a white towel,
and sat on the balcony to let the sunlight dry my wet hair. I wanted to feel
the intimacy of two elements

interacting. I wanted to tell you why I loved you, but I could only point
at a tree.

Once, This Forest Belonged to a Storm

Enter quietly. Here is the broken pine branch, heavy with moss. The birds have returned, but they sing an octave higher now.

We should have left a bucket out, let it fill with rainwater, then measured it, the way ancient Jewish mystics tried to measure the dimensions of God.

Might It Not Be That We Have Appointments to Keep in the Past

> And might it not be, continued Austerlitz, that we also have appointments
> to keep in the past, in what has gone before and is for the most part
> extinguished, and we must go there in search of places and people who
> have some connection with us on the far side of time, so to speak?
> —W. G. Sebald, *Austerlitz*

I

Midsummer. A night of fitful sleep.

The dream in which you are not you, your house is not your house.

Childhood: a girl with her ear to the floor who can only hear one half
of the story.

I remember my father at the front door,

back from abroad,

while my mother drifted into the bedroom,

and the Hanukkah candles burned down to their wick,

how everything was always ending,

even as it was beginning, every arrival was preparation

for being left. Poem: a letter that says, *come back, come back*, in the language
of a crow.

This morning, I sit on the edge of my bed and think of what is far away:

my grandmother's body curled into the prow of a ship,

my great-grandmother walking slowly

through the cemetery as snow falls in the linden trees

in Berlin . . .

Back then, death was acknowledged by holding an egg in the palm of your hand.

It was believed that the soul of the deceased could be transferred to the egg.

Then, you ate the egg.

I am the silence that follows after silence. I am a stone that has landed,

by chance, between a patch of monkshood and wild huckleberries—

II
There is a place I go when you go to sleep

a meadow

where all day long, the soil stores the sun's heat and then, at night, releases it.

Here, there is a lake, filtered for centuries by volcanic rock, so clear
it can induce vertigo.

Instead of love, God is patience:

the time it takes a snail to make its way across a forest path.

I remember

retreating up the stairs, into my childhood bedroom

to read a book my father gave me with all the German names for family:
die Mutter, der Vater,

die Schwester, der Bruder. I remember

wanting the words to mean something

to me, but they lived on the other side of time, vast sections of which were
impassable.

There is a place I go when you go to sleep,

at the hinge of a Hebrew hour,

which is of no fixed length.

Take the last bus out of the city.

Watch the streetlights, one by one, going dark.

Here is the whale bone that sits on my father's writing desk, emblem
of his loneliness—

The Archdruid

Here, girls read magazines out loud to one another.
Boys drink beer and jump into the sea. Their knees and toes are purple.

I am next to you, but I cannot see you.

You are like the white glare of a spaceship.

One time you and I saw a wild buffalo on the side of the road. We pulled over
to watch it eat. I remember I could hear you breathing.

You moved away from the city because you were always cold.

People are lonely places, you said.

Here, we buy tickets and wait in line for entry.
Time is doled out in silver droplets.

We sit on long stretches of sand and face forward. We plant trees
inside museums and watch them grow.

As a boy, you once cracked open a butterfly chrysalis to hurry it along.
The word *species* meant nothing to you then.

I am like you. Houses stare at me like the faces of policemen.

I often go days without touching anyone.

Migration

Feasting on carrot leaves and honeysuckle,

        on hollyhock and cabbage,

darting between tangles of telephone wire,

        the color of fire seen through the stained-glass window

of a cathedral,

    mythic-green, paradox-blue, some with seven orange spots,

like pages ripped from the memoir of a rainbow,

        classified by size or sex, born in late September,

early June,

      butterflies, billions,

in parking lots where mothers pick up their children,

        in markets where vendors sell cherries,

tumbling, catapulting,

      like lilacs blooming without water, like life

without the possibility of life. They remind me

      of the red dust which settles

on the porches and plazas

        of Seville, or the blue cotton dress I've carried with me

from house to house, from Los Angeles

      to San Francisco—

in gardens and on gravestones,

        rising like the soul of my grandfather, born by the name

of Avram, changed to Lawrence

        when he was twelve. (The last time I saw him

was in a hospital. After, my sister and I sat in the car

        and listened to country songs;

silver sunlight poured through the window.)

        They go north,

where the first frost comes from, where my parents came from,

        beaver and fir and moss-covered stone,

green breeding more green,

        wounds that can only be healed

by their own perpetrators, tooth of a wolf, hair of a witch,

        land of rain on the roof of a synagogue

permanently closed,

        rain on the rhododendrons my grandmother tends each year

when the white sky breaks,

        and she remembers, for a moment, her grandfather:

Vienna, 1933,

        he bought her a red balloon which she let slip

from her fingers, over the ruins of a burned-down barn

made from the wood of a thousand-year-old pine,

past the abandoned train tracks

filled with desert sage

and wild dandelion,

past the mound where a man is buried with his watch still running:

they are

an expression of exile, like the deep enduring sound

a blue whale makes in captivity

or the chorus-less songs of those forced to flee

to the mountains. California Sister, Ox-Eyed Satyr,

sliding across silk reams of light, a display of whim

and warm air,

Monarch, Painted Lady, Western White,

sputtering, inefficient, on their way toward

somewhere else,

Duskywing, Silver-Spotted Skipper—

like ash a man says in the garden

where he sits with his new wife, they have just planted

a pear tree, they want to have a baby, they have painted the baby's room

the colors of the pear tree—

burning, burning—

Natural Disaster

No one thought it could happen, not like this.
The experts were speechless.

For once, they knew only as much as anybody else.

The public was advised to remain indoors.
They cooked dinner, lit candles, drifted farther
and farther apart, as if each in his own rowboat on a black sea.

When it was over, they crawled out of their houses,
wary of their experience, staring at the neighbors.

What could they deduce from the rubble?
They touched it, as if that certified something.

The whole city had a green tint like an underwater kingdom.

Wasn't this what they always wanted?
Wasn't this some private wish fulfilled?

They stood at its center, lifted like a bride and groom.
The metal core around which the soft world rotates.

Soon the children invented a game called Victims and Heroes.
It became harder and harder to look at those they loved.

A New World

We knew it wouldn't last. The sky was the last page in a book
and we could see it turning.

We heard church bells ringing inside us
and the world opened like a shattered diamond, producing a clarity
that made the sidewalks shimmer.

      It had the hush of a forest after a tree falls.
The quiet of dust settling. Of birds finding a new branch on which to perch.
The reorganization that must take place when a thing that was no longer is.

The light was like the light in a fairy tale
when the woman who has been sleeping for a century suddenly wakes up.

It was a world in which animals could heal their wounds themselves,
God had decided that.

We knew it wouldn't last. The sky was the last page in a book
and we could see it turning.

Erinnerung

When I was born, my great-grandmother called my parents to find out whether or not I had blue eyes. This was important to her. She believed her blue eyes were the means by which she had survived. You look just like her, my father says to me years later in a restaurant. My body, too, is an heirloom.

Creation Myth

In the beginning, there was only darkness.

Not the dark of the prairie at night,
fireflies nestled like hot pearls in the grass.

More like the sense of something
approaching, weaving a black basket in the sky.

Days came and went without epiphany.
Then the world began to materialize.

It was like coming down out
of the clouds in an airplane:
miles of snow-scented wheat,
white-tailed deer and wild turkey.

The people had a feeling
that somewhere their lives were already lived.

They heard a narrator
in the cornfield, a voice like a flashlight
in the barn of the future.

Meeting Shakespeare

I met Shakespeare in a hotel room downtown.
There was a lamp on by the bed and the radio was playing.
Shakespeare was wearing a gold watch and a velvet sash; it was clear
he had a taste for beautiful things.
He sat in a chair and let me talk and I told him about television and strip malls,
how I have the same blue eyes
as my mother. Why do we inherit what hurts us? I asked,
but he didn't answer.
I went to the bathroom. I looked in the mirror.
I imagined what it would be like to be a woman living four hundred years
in the future who was imagining
what it would be like to be a woman living four hundred years in the past.
I washed my hands. I reentered the room.
Outside, the night was a bucket with a hole in the bottom,
the darkness kept spilling out.
Shakespeare, I said, sometimes when I'm sad, I don't feel anything at all.
He put his hand on my shoulder.
He was a tactful man. *Very good*, he said and was gone.

Instructions

Start with description.
Talk about the dark of the desert, the way the stars are grooves cut by ice skates.
Pretend it was November.
Decide that the wind came from a storm in the sea.
Imagine your mother was asleep,
dreaming about foxes. Tell us that a slot machine is just a night-blooming flower.
Tell us that deer are drawn to salt because they believe it will change them.
Then say *people never learn their lesson and that's why they write poems*.
Now fix your gaze on a beetle.
Tell us that nothing could possibly exist beyond this beetle.
Explain that even if something *did* exist beyond this beetle, it would be irrelevant.
Confirm your theory by repeating it again in a different language.
Leave no room for argument.

Major Arcana

Some words are transparent, others are opaque. *Seizure.* No matter how hard I look I will never see inside it.

I used to sneak into her room and try on her clothes. On her dresser, pills, a glass bottle of perfume, a silk dress printed with roses, limp in my hands, that I slipped my small body into. As if one sister's suffering could be exchanged for another, like shuffling a deck of cards.

Memoir

In third grade, I gave a report on a starfish. In fourth grade, I learned to believe my own lies. One night, I was visited by angels while I slept. They were dressed in blue robes and taught me their word for "thank you," but had no word for "I." In fifth grade, I became afraid of fire.

~

I moved to a town on an island. It was illegal to borrow a pencil or talk about your dreams. Once, a doctor with dark hair asked me to rate my sadness from one to ten, with ten being the most sad I've ever felt and one being the least sad. Instead of music, the radio played the sounds of storms.

~

I swam in rivers. I climbed volcanoes. In Berlin, I drank spiced wine at a Christmas market under the light of a star-shaped lantern. I lost my glasses in a museum and wandered blindly through the Impressionists.

~

I think telephone wires are beautiful. I believe clumsiness is an emotional state. I know nothing about the life cycle of bats. I do know how to draw a mermaid. I like to cut my sandwiches in half so I can see the inside. I wish I knew the names of all my bones.

~

One night, I met a magician. He specialized in teleportation; one moment we were on the beach with the sun on our faces and the next we were in a crowded café opening cans of beer. We fell in love. We moved to San Francisco. We had a plant that grew so big it fell over and died.

~

Then, strange things started to happen. I woke up each morning with grass stains on my knees. I knew what people were going to say before they said it.

~

You have too much air in your lungs, a singer said. Your aura is broken, a fortuneteller said. Once a week, spend twenty-two minutes and forty-five seconds staring at the color blue without blinking, a painter said. Drink a bottle of wine by yourself at midnight, a poet said.

~

I began to work in a tropical fish store. We sold fish in every color of the rainbow. The store had no windows and I read Aristotle by the light of the aquariums.

~

On my walk home, I met a Romanticist in the woods. She had curly red hair and seemed to be in a hurry. I have a problem, I said, I don't know where to put my hands. Try laughing and crying at the same time, she said.

~

I built a house on an empty plot where nothing grew except weeds. I built a wood fence around the house. Then I built a brick wall around the fence around the house. Then I planted tall topiaries of holly and laurel around the wall around the fence around the house. To keep the nighttime out! I shouted to the magician who stood staring at me from the doorstep.

~

In town, the clouds were disappearing. The mayor launched an investigation. Whoever is responsible for this crime will be punished, he said. He was wearing a misbuttoned coat while orating loudly from a podium.

~

That night, the number 72 came to me in a dream. I took this to mean that, in 72 weeks, I would have another dream, in which I would be visited by the ghost of a happy shepherd, who would then recount for me his dream, in which I would finally discover the essence of who I really am.

~

I thought of myself as a lone wolf, living off the scraps of my own perceptions, but I worried that other people saw me as an outdated map, in which all the countries are divided the wrong way.

~

I believe the word "unfettered" should refer to a bird molting its feathers. I have a fear of high noon. Other people's handwriting makes me weep. I have a theory that the air is made of invisible lenses, and whenever they line up, you can see that people are, for the most part, good.

Memories of a Time We Don't Remember

We hadn't brushed our teeth or combed our hair
when we found ourselves

deposited at the door of the world
like an unmarked package.

The sky was grey so we were unable to discern time passing.
It might have been hours

or maybe years. We alone held the key to a room we would never find,
the map of a country that no longer exists.

Although we tried,
sipping coffee and brainstorming, comparing pie charts,

sitting through endless therapy sessions.
We even considered writing a memoir.

It's like the story about the girl who picks stars from the sky
and gathers them in her skirt.

A story about our wish to hold things
that can't be held.

Conversations with Angels

I have so many questions, but I'm scared to ask them. Are you scared to answer them?

Yes.

The rabbi said love is knowledge. The more we know about people the more we love them. I felt this the other day when I went to karaoke. I was watching a girl sing and dance in the green and red disco light and I felt that loved her. I also realized I have never let my guard down in public, have never let myself be known. There is always a smaller version of me, crouched, hiding.

How much did you have to drink?

I was sober.

Well, maybe that was the problem.

When I was up late last night on the internet, I read that twenty percent of Ashkenazi Jews are descended from just four women. That's why we carry so many genetic mutations. We're still passing down the legacy of our near obliteration.

I didn't know that.

I thought our bodies were personal, the one place on earth that was truly ours.

Have you ever felt that way about your body?

No. I've been thinking about the painting by Gerhard Richter of his wife, Ema. She's naked, descending a staircase, the moment right after they learned she was pregnant. Her eyes are downcast, knees bent.

The Hasidim believed knees were holy, that's why we bend them in prayer.

Then staircases must be holy places.

Yesterday, I was walking down a staircase built in the 1920s before cars or roads, bougainvillea on one side and an avocado tree on the other. I felt I was standing on a bridge between what has been said and what would be said, touching both.

Isn't that always true?

Maybe. I like the word wingspan, but I wonder if there's a better word that describes the sound of air being displaced when a bird takes flight.

Maybe you can make one up.

When my sister was pregnant, she bought a lamp that cycles through the colors of the rainbow; she said she wanted to name the child Lavender. Is naming an act of tenderness or aggression?

Would it make you uncomfortable if the answer was both?

Yes.

On Belonging

I've been
banished
from the
kingdom
of the living.
I see them
walking
their dogs
and expressing
themselves
to people they
love. I want
in like everybody
else. At least
lend me
a book about it,
trade me
your
dinner plans,
your moon
like a
breathing hole
in the black box
of night.
I promise
to give it all
back.
I'm tired
of deciding
which side
not to be on.
Remember
our cat in
California.
The way
she wandered
in and out

of the house
however
she pleased.
She swam
between
those
two worlds
seamlessly.
Not like
one was some
sacrifice
for the other.

City of Angels

It was Wednesday

and I was making the interminable walk through a city
that kept repeating itself:
house, car, gate, house, car, gate, house, car, gate—

the truth is I was deeply depressed. All of a sudden

I saw a red neon sign glowing on the street corner
like jewels

in the palm of an angel

and the angel was singing a song which made the color of the night
turn from black to indigo
as if the sky were smoldering

the way hot coals come back to life if you blow on them—

the doctor says I suffer from a poison which I administer to myself
in retribution for my own joy
if you can believe that.

Which means

I wrote the song that the angel was singing to me
I am the angel—

Seventh Meditation on the Existence of God

It's the thing that happened that was never solved.
It's the thing that happened that was solved
years later on an apple farm outside of town. It was somebody's birthday,
the bus broke down, and an animal swept across the sky.
Then it hid inside a vowel sung by a woman in a bar at midnight.
That's when it led me to its secret chamber.

Now it sighs; it's become self-conscious.
Now it's humming because it hasn't got the words.
Now it's telling me its middle name, which it's never told anyone.
When it says pain, it means all pain.
When it says longing, it means every type of longing.
It's stored in a golden vessel in the shape of a cat with sapphire eyes.

It can only be thought of from the inside.
At dusk, it disappears in an explosion of screeching blue light;
that's why we're all so sad,
that's why we stare into empty cups.
You can still find it in a motel room in Wyoming while the TV plays softly,
and you look in the mirror and notice how you've changed.

Quarantine

Chopin on the stereo. A bag of flour on the kitchen counter.
The lamp emits a thin tremble
of light. We are stirring olive oil with onions

in a steel pan and I am thinking of my Oma in 1938
on the telephone with the Swiss embassy, her daughter in a hospital bed
with diphtheria while the war went on, then sailing

across the ocean to America with a piece of rye bread
in her wool pocket. I am thinking about foresight, how it means
arriving at the moment before the moment

arrives. I am thinking of walking through a forest, how the spaces
between trees widen like telescopes. Once
my father and I rode up a chairlift in the middle of a blizzard,

then skied down toward a city we believed in but could not see.
I am thinking of the white cloud of the present.
I am thinking of a time before newspapers or windows

or the idea of heaven. I am thinking of magnetic fields, the raw material
of mountains. I stand up. I take the hand of the person I love.
Is it true that only time can tell? I ask but don't wait for an answer.

He has entered the room like a stray cat sheltering from a storm.
We will sit at a wood table encased in a circle
of light, saying the names of flowers that we know, and repeating them.

Gedächtnis

Before A. could talk, her mother ventriloquized for her, as if she were a doll, pretended she was saying things she wasn't really saying. What mother is ventriloquizing for me right now? I drive all night, passing gas stations and diners, believing that distance in space equals distance in time.

Not Sad & Not Beautiful

A car is spinning out of control
        in a snowy field. There's a stillness at the center of it.
We call this stillness ordinary life.
        Only the angels know this.

They sit at a table drinking boiled fennel and reading books.
        They are reading about the history of chaos,
a word which once meant the void
        at the beginning of the universe, a rift between heaven and earth.

The Greeks personified it.
        According to Hesiod, Chaos was the oldest god.
Gaius Julius Hyginus, a Roman, said Chaos was born from Mist,
        but his books are filled with errors.

The angels are exhausted. They don't understand.
        They look out the window at the city
with its movie marquees and earnest sidewalks. Its teenagers
        confessing love to one another on striped blankets at beaches

in the sun. They notice what happens
        when moisture from the sea combines with heat
from the desert to create light that fills the air
        with a starry resin. The angels think that there are two kinds

of dying: one which is sad and beautiful,
        and the other, which is not sad and not beautiful,
but merely a redistribution of weight. A shifting from one foot
        to another. The angels have terrible eyesight

on account of all the books. They have become myopic.
        To them, the earth looks like slow green rain.

Palm Reader

I have done what I knew I would. I have risen
not from the sea,
        but from a blue-green swimming pool,
clean and dripping, one arm reaching
for a warm towel. Unlike the characters in Russian novels
seized by sudden illness, trapped in bodies
they never knew they were bound to,
        I am capable of reincarnation.
I have fallen asleep again in my black and gold dress,
        crumpled like a bird's nest beneath my weight,
as if night were a thing that never happened.
Each man wakes in the morning and sees the sky, a writer says.
        Instead, I see a crime scene
between Normandie and Western, sectioned off
with yellow tape, as if some part of this world could remain
        unchanged. I do not like freeways.
I miss the trains of the East, their structured narratives,
the taximeters twitching like insect wings, red reminders
of where I've been.
        I am not what I am. All the old hotels
have fallen to their knees,
        but I see one chandelier still swinging,
casting shattered light along the wall
like cave paintings, jasmine-scented ghosts of the Cocoanut Grove.
Land of rolling hills and arrivals, of ceaseless exodus.

Autobiography

You were born in Los Angeles
in 1987

Ten months in the womb, is the story your mother likes to tell
as if you loved her
so much you didn't want to leave

But it's not true; you love
living

In the summer, she took you to the beach with an umbrella and bowl of cherries
but you preferred the flux

of autumn or spring
before the weather had settled into one season or another

and when you kissed yourself in the mirror
you were both the boy and the girl, like the agave producing its own sugar

You are who you were

when you rolled up your jeans to wade knee-deep in the river, milk-white,
containing minerals from the mountains

To give and to receive are one action, you think

You want
now what you wanted
then:

your poem in someone else's hands, flowers at the end of winter,
confused for snow

ACKNOWLEDGMENTS

I would like to thank the editors of the journals in which these poems, sometimes in altered form, first appeared:

Adroit Journal: "The Undrowned World"
AGNI: "Natural Disaster"
Cimarron Review: "Ein Sof," "A New World"
H.O.W. Journal: "On Belonging"
Indiana Review: "Palm Reader"
Iowa Review: "Getting Ready"
Los Angeles Review: "Interrogation"
Los Angeles Review of Books: "Against Daytime"
Minnesota Review: "Threat from Above"
Narrative: "The Outlaw"
North American Review: "Not Sad & Not Beautiful"
Plume: "Meeting Shakespeare"
Poetry Northwest: "San Fernando Valley, 1999"
Rattle: "Dear Husband"
Salmagundi: "Notes on Flying"
Sewanee Review: "Instructions," "Migration," "Nocturne"
Smartish Pace: "Dear Husband," "Theory of Nature"
Southern Review: "In Defense of Daytime," "Memoir"
Two Peach: "Dinner Party in Outer Space," "Memories of a Time I Don't
     Remember"
Zyzzyva: "The Archdruid," "City of Angels," "Creation Myth," "The Visit"
32 Poems: "Seventh Meditation on the Existence of God"

Thank you to my parents for their love and support. And to Elizabeth Metzger, Sara Freeman, Sam Ross, C. J. A., Katharine Ogle, Stephanie Horvath, Essy Stone, Muriel Leung, and especially Catherine Pond, for their sensitivity and insight in reading early drafts of this manuscript. Thanks as well to Alexandria Hall, Erin Lynch, Michelle Orsi, and Callie Siskel, who offered me invaluable feedback on individual poems.

I am very grateful to Ellen Doré Watson for selecting this manuscript from a pile of anonymous submissions. And to everyone at the University of Massachusetts Press for their care in bringing this book into the world.

Special thanks to my teachers, David St. John, Susan McCabe, Maggie Nelson, Richard Howard, Lucie Brock-Broido, Josh Bell, and Laurie Sheck, for their wisdom and guidance. And to my early teachers for encouraging me: Eavan Boland, Robert Pinsky, Michael McGriff, and Elizabeth Bradfield. Thank you to the Djerassi Resident Artists Program, Bread Loaf Writers' Conference, and Hedgebrook Writer-in-Residence Program for the time and space to write. Thank you to Adam Ross of the *Sewanee Review* for championing my writing. And to Paisley Rekdal, whose discerning eye helped me shape this book into its current form. My deepest gratitude to Dr. G., without whom the book would not exist.

Thank you to my brother. Thank you to my sister for everything.

Thank you to my grandmothers.

This book is dedicated in part to Mark Strand, my professor and mentor, whose voice is indelible in my mind.

And to Will Alden. Thank you for the hours you've spent poring over these pages, for long drives through Los Angeles while I sort out my feelings. And for your unwavering belief that I could, in fact, write a love poem.

NOTES

The lines about imaginary numbers in "Love Poem" refer to a passage in
The Confusions of Young Törless by Robert Musil.

The poem "Dear Husband" refers to a *Fresh Air* interview with the conductor
Yannick Nézet-Séguin in which he says about the opening chords of
Beethoven's Symphony No. 5, "It's Beethoven not knowing where
this is all going."

The title of "Seven Meditations on the Existence of God" was inspired by
René Descartes's "Meditations on First Philosophy," which consists
of six meditations proving the existence of God.

The title of "Not Sad & Not Beautiful" was inspired by a passage in *Magic
Mountain* by Thomas Mann.

The last line of the poem "Interrogation" was inspired by the last line of
Joan Didion's *Book of Common Prayer*, in which she writes, "I have not
been the witness I wanted to be."

The poem "The Archdruid" is dedicated to the environmentalist David
Brower. In John McPhee's book *Encounters with the Archdruid*, he writes
that Brower, as a child, once broke open a chrysalis in an attempt to
help the butterfly emerge.

The Gerhard Richter painting referred to in "Conversations with Angels"
is *Ema (Akt auf einer Treppe)*.

In the poem "Palm Reader," the line "I am not what I am" is borrowed from
a speech by Iago in William Shakespeare's *Othello*.

In the poem "Dedication," the idea that a worm could have a "truer
understanding of the universe" was inspired by a section in Annie
Dillard's *Pilgrim at Tinker Creek*. The Yiddish sayings are sourced from
Johanna Kovitz's YiddishWit.com.

I first encountered many of the Hasidic beliefs referred to in this book
in Gershom Scholem's *Major Trends in Jewish Mysticism* and *On the
Kabbalah and Its Symbolism*.

JUNIPER
JUNIPER PRIZE FOR POETRY

This volume is the fifty-first recipient of the
Juniper Prize for Poetry, established in 1975 by
University of Massachusetts Press in collaboration with
the UMass Amherst MFA program for Poets and Writers.
The prize is named in honor of the poet Robert Francis
(1901–1987), who for many years lived in Fort Juniper,
a tiny home of his own construction, in Amherst.